growing Lavender

A GUIDE FOR COOLER CLIMATES
BY CHRISTINE MOORE

Epic Press

Belleville, Ontario, Canada

GROWING LAVENDER
Copyright © 2004, Christine Moore

Illustrations by Greg Beettam,
Time Bucket Graphics, Toronto

Library and Archives Canada Cataloguing in Publication
Moore, Christine, 1956-
    Growing lavender : a guide for colder climates / Christine
Moore.
  ISBN 1-55306-789-4
    1. Lavenders. I. Title.
SB317.L37M66 2004   635.9'3396   C2004-903357-3

**For more information or
to order additional copies, please contact:**
Christine Moore
116 Belsize Drive
Toronto, ON
M4S 1L7
growing-lavender.com

Epic Press is an imprint of *Essence Publishing*.
For more information, contact:
20 Hanna Court, Belleville, Ontario, Canada K8P 5J2.
Phone: 1-800-238-6376 • Fax: (613) 962-3055.
E-mail: publishing@essencegroup.com
Internet: www.essencegroup.com

TABLE OF CONTENTS

ACKNOWLEDGEMENTS

Sincere thanks to:

My mother, Marjorie Moore,
for encouraging my expeditions.

Diane Fisk, who asked me if I'd thought
about lavender, and launched this journey.

Joan Head, Editor of *The Lavender Bag*.

Mary Godfrey and Norfolk Lavender in England.

David Christie, Jersey Island Lavender.

Christina Ritchie and Humber Nurseries,
Woodbridge, Ontario.

The gardeners who so freely shared their
successes and failures with me.

And always, Auntie Jean.

FOREWORD

L avender is one of the most satisfying plants
to grow. It asks for little, yet rewards us with
an abundance of fragrant flowers in a variety of
colours. Even when the plant is not in bloom,
fragrance lingers in the foliage. The popularity
of lavender continues to increase as it is suitable
for a variety of gardens: herb gardens, healing
gardens, culinary gardens, cut flower gardens,
rock gardens, and dried flower gardens.

There has been little research on the frost
hardiness of varieties. I certainly do not intend
this book to be the final work on growing
lavender in climates where part of the year is
below freezing. It is my hope to demystify the
plants' names and to help you select varieties to
enjoy in your home and garden. Much of the
information supplied is from Canadian and
American gardeners and my own experimenta-
tion. The *cooler climates* in the title refers to
winter hardiness, as summer (July and August)
in much of Canada can reach a lavender-loving
28–35 degrees C.

1

THE LAVENDER FAMILY

Lavender belongs to a family of plants called *Lamiacea*. Family members are described as strongly aromatic, small, evergreen shrubs with lance-shaped or linear-shaped leaves. They are characterized by "lipped" flowers. These are flowers in which one petal is a different shape and often a different colour from the remaining petals. This is part of the flower's way to attract insects for pollination. Roses, zinnias, and daylilies are examples of flowers which are not lipped. Their flowers and petals are symmetrical in shape. Look at the stems of a lavender plant. They tend to be square, as do other *Lamiacea* family members including rosemary, thyme, basil, and sage. In plant classification, families are further broken down into genus, then species, then variety. Within each grouping, plants become more similar. Lavender belongs to the genus *Lavandula*. While native to the Mediterranean, it is also found on the Canary Islands in the west, and as far away as Arabia and India in the east. Many varieties thrive in dry soils and some at high mountain altitudes in France and Switzerland.

There are believed to be thirty-two to thirty-six species in the *Lavandula* genus. Within those species are over one hundred different varieties. DNA research is ongoing and as more is learned, the classifications may continue to change. Unfortunately, most lavenders are not frost hardy. The species *Lavandula angustifolia*, commonly called *English lavender*, contains varieties most suited to cooler climates. Hybrids of *Lavandula angustifolia* and *Lavandula latifolia* produce many commercial varieties and some of these, as we will see later, are also frost hardy.

WHAT'S IN A NAME?

How the name *lavender* originated is not known. Some believe it came from the Latin *lavare* which means *to wash*. This theory says that the Romans, very fond of their baths, used lavender to scent their bathing water. A series of articles by Anthony Lyman-Dixon of Arne Herbs in Great Britain, examined the introduction of lavender to England. He states,

> Because the Latin for bath is *lavacrum,* and for dirty washing, *lavandaria*, it was assumed that the Latin-speaking Romans invented the term for the plant... Actually, I have been unable to find any reference whatever to lavender in the Roman classics, nor in the *Materia medica* of the great mediaeval teaching hospital at Salerno.[1]

Others suggest the name was derived from the Latin *livere*, to be livid, or bluish in colour. There is an expression,

---

[1] Anthony Lyman-Dixon. "Did the Tudors Invent Lavender?" *The Lavender Bag*, November 2000, p. 17.

"to be livid with rage," in which *livid* means to be furious. As early herbalists used lavender to calm people and treat mental problems, *livere* could have been the origin of the word. In fact much of the ancient history of lavender is a mystery, and many of the ancient sources are not verifiable.

The Bible has several references to a precious ointment made with *nard, essence of nard* or *spikenard*. In the past, lavender had the common name *spike lavender* and therefore some people felt it was the *nard* of the Bible. Herbalists generally agree the plant referred to is *Nardostachys jatamansi*, native to the Himalayan Mountains, widely exported and very expensive.

2

WINTER SURVIVAL

WHAT MAKES A PLANT FROST HARDY?

You leave a tender plant outside on a cold night and the next morning it is a sad sight. Limp, it wilts and dies. Yet other plants don't seem to notice the cold. The difference is how the plant handles water within its cells. In plants that are not frost hardy, when the temperature dips below freezing, the water held within the plant cells freezes, forming ice crystals. Ice occupies more space than water. The cell wall stretches in an effort to accommodate the ice. The effort is futile and the cell wall ruptures. As the temperature rises, the ice crystals melt. The cell walls, now damaged, can no longer hold the water and other cell contents. The cell cannot function properly and it dies. If the damage is extensive, the plant dies. Frost hardy plants have the ability to alter the water inside the cell with naturally occurring chemicals that prevent the cell water from freezing. No ice forms and the cells do not rupture. Plants either have this ability or they do not.

Winter survival may be affected by snow cover as snow provides a layer of insulation to plants. Perennial plants survive our cold winters best under a deep blanket of snow. While the wind-chill may dip to -15C, a plant buried under snow is insulated and protected from temperature extremes and temperature fluctuations. Cold air is usually dry air. A good snow cover will also prevent plants from drying out in a cold wind.

Within some gardens are microclimates. A microclimate refers to an area in which temperature extremes are different than commonly occur in your zone. You may live in Zone 5, but have a corner in the garden where Zone 6 plants winter successfully. These areas are usually protected; often by walls, buildings, or hedges. A change in topography, such as a slope or valley, may also promote a microclimate and allow plants to over-winter that would otherwise die.

Artificial protection helps some plants—roses for example. Often we insulate them with collars filled with soil, or mound soil around the base of the plant. Passionate growers cover their roses using a wooden frame built over the bed and covered with polystyrene. These protective measures take the place of a good blanket of snow. Some gardeners cover lavender plants with extra soil, leaves, and straw and find they can occasionally over-winter varieties which are otherwise marginal for their zone.

FINDING YOUR ZONE

There are maps which show the lowest average winter temperature for an area. Garden catalogues or nurseries often include a zone map for customer convenience. Agriculture Canada produced a new map in 2003. You will find it on the Internet at http://www.agr.gc.ca and search the term *zone hardiness map.* In the United States, the Web address is http://www.usna.usda.gov/hardzone. Your local library should also be able to find you a current map.

3

LAVENDER IN THE GARDEN

Few plants are as versatile or undemanding as lavender. The primary requirements are a well-drained soil, and above all, plenty of sun. A wet spring during which lavender roots sit in damp ground can mean death to the plants, even though they survived the cold winter. If you are planting in clay soil, it is suggested you dig a hole at least 30 cm (12") deep and round. Fill with a mixture of 50/50 soil and sand, or soil and horticultural grit, to improve the drainage. Lavender also does well in raised beds. A pH between 6 and 8 is the optimum. The section "Fertilizing Lavender" will provide further details. Once soil and sun requirements are met, lavender will thrive in a variety of situations.

PLANT ALONG A PATHWAY

The plants appreciate the heat reflected from the walkway.

ROCK GARDEN

Smaller varieties such as *L.a.* 'Hidcote,' *L.a.* 'Munstead,' *L.a.* 'Lady,' *L.a.* 'Rosea' do well in rock gardens.

THEMED GARDENS

Try butterfly gardens, Victorian gardens, herb gardens, informal gardens, or scented gardens.

There are white-flowering varieties, such as *L. angustifolia* 'Alba,' which are perfect additions to white flower gardens.

FORMAL GARDEN

The dwarf varieties can be trimmed to form a neat hedge in a formal garden.

SUNNY COURTYARD GARDEN

Lavender can be planted with other sun-loving perennials such as: *achilles* (the yellow varieties would look great with purple lavender), *penstemon*, salvia, *santolina,* sedum, *Stachys lanata*, lemon verbena, bergamot, and *artemesia.*

Sun-loving annuals that grow well with lavender include: petunias, geraniums, sunflowers (plant tall varieties behind the lavender), marigolds, zinnias, *portulaca*, and nasturtiums.

SMALL GARDENS

In a small garden, lavender is ideal. When space is at a premium, it is important that plants give multi-season interest. Lavender blooms several times each year, and the foliage is attractive and scented year-round. I have been treated to a refreshing whiff as my snow-laden shovel brushes a plant near the walkway when I am moving snow.

MULCH

Mulching is usually done to control weeds and to keep the soil under the mulch moist. If you wish to mulch lavender for weed control, try using pea gravel or white sand applied to a depth of 3–4 cm (1/2–1"). Mulching lavender with bark, peat moss, or woodchips is not recommended. These mulches keep the soil too wet. Peat moss also increases soil acidity, which does not promote good lavender growth.

4

FERTILIZING LAVENDER

Lavender will grow and bloom quite nicely when it is completely neglected. In nature, it will thrive in rocky outcrops where you can't imagine it receives any nutrition at all. Between my home and my neighbour's is a narrow 30-cm (12")-wide strip of land. It has a very steep south-facing slope and for years had been home to a variety of weeds. We decided to plant a selection of *L. angustifolia* 'Hidcote' and *L. angustifolia* 'Munstead' in an effort to establish a small hedge. This spot has several good features: blistering day-long sun and excellent drainage. The soil was like cement. When dry, it was so hard a trowel would not dent it. Once the weeds were removed we added a little potting soil, which actually made no difference to the soil's cement-like quality, and we planted the lavender. All survived the winter and bloomed the following year, but the plants quickly developed a loose, spreading appearance. The stems were thick and woody. The difference between these plants and the textbook-perfect lavender plants a few feet away was startling. The "perfect plants" share a raised bed with roses. This has led me to believe that better soil and a little feeding will produce better flowering plants and perhaps discourage early woody growth. Using a 7-7-7 fertilizer in the spring will give your plants a nutritional boost, without overfeeding.

WHY DO WE FEED PLANTS?

We feed the plants to provide nutrition for healthy growth. The primary nutrients we add are:

1. Nitrogen: Fuels leafy growth and is the N symbol on the bag.

2. Phosphorus: Encourages flower and fruit formation and is the P symbol on the bag.

3. Potassium: Helps plants form healthy roots and is the K symbol on the bag; it is often in the form of potash.

These three nutrients appear in the order above on fertilizers. A 7-7-7 fertilizer refers to a mixture that is 7% available nitrogen, 7% available phosphate and 7% available potassium. A fertilizer with the numbers 15-30-15 is a mixture that is 15% available nitrogen, 30% available phosphate, and 15% available potassium. It is usually reserved for flowers or vegetables that bloom the entire season and require more nutrition than lavender. If new growth on your lavender plants is yellow instead of green, there could be an iron deficiency. A number of general purpose fertilizers now include iron.

Compost can be gold to your garden soil. It provides organic matter and soil bacteria, which help make fertilizer available for the plant to absorb. It also loosens heavy clay soil, can increase the water-holding capacity, and decrease pH. Lavender does not require it. However, if your young lavender plants show poor growth, adding compost may help improve the general growing conditions.

WHAT ABOUT pH?

This is a scale for measuring how acid or alkaline a soil is. The scale is from zero to 14. A pH of 7 is neutral. Below 7 is acid. The lower the number, the more acidic the soil is. Above 7 is alkaline. The higher the number, the more alkaline the soil. Soil pH can easily be measured with inexpensive testing strips available at most garden centres. Some plants, like azaleas and rhododendrons, need an acidic soil in which to thrive. Lavender prefers soil in the 6 to 8 range. Lime, or correctly, dolomitic limestone, is very alkaline and can be added to soil to raise the pH if needed. If you have a sandy alkaline area where nothing will grow, then lavender should spring to mind as a possibility. Peat moss will lower the soil pH and is therefore not recommended for use around lavender. For the average gardener, pH is not really a concern when planting lavender. If you have tried several lavender plants in the same area and they just will not grow, checking the pH may give you the answer.

ROSES AND LAVENDER

These are unlikely bedfellows. As mentioned, lavender prefers a soil pH of 6 to 8. Roses prefer a pH on the acid side of 5.8 to 6.2. Lavender was thought at one time to repel insects from roses, but I know of no study confirming this. Roses are also heavy feeders, requiring regular fertilizing throughout the growing season. Too much fertilizer on lavender will promote leggy, non-blooming growth. Roses require plenty of water; lavender does not. That said, I have

L. angustifolia 'Hidcote,' *L. angustifolia* 'Alba,' and *L x intermedia* 'Provence' growing beautifully at the front of my rose bed. The bed is raised and basks in full sun all day. The bed is watered with a soaker hose near the roses, away from the lavender; and the roses, not the lavender, receive the fertilizer. In photos of older gardens showing lavender and roses together, the roses are not usually modern hybrid teas, but varieties which require less feeding and tolerate dryer soils. They are certainly beautiful companions; simply be aware of specific needs.

5

PRUNING LAVENDER

Pruning lavender will help it live longer and produce better flowers. Know the variety of lavender you have planted and the size it will naturally attain. If the variety is large, like *L. x intermedia* 'Grosso,' do not prune it to make it stay small. The growth and flower production will be affected. Letting a small variety like *L. angustifolia* 'Munstead' grow too large will encourage woody horizontal growth and affect blooming. Long woody stems are also prone to breaking under heavy snow. Read the tags that come with your plants, and prune to maintain their optimum size.

We tend to think perennials will last forever. Lavender is certainly long-lived, yet you may find the flowering quality declines after seven or eight years. That is the time to replace the plant. If your plant has long woody stems, there is not much you can do but replace it. If it is an old favourite, you can try taking some softwood cuttings. We will cover this in the section "Propagating Lavender." Occasionally a plant may be pruned to a much smaller size and it will sprout new growth. This should only be done as a last resort, as you risk killing the plant. There are two schools of thought regarding when to prune lavender. Lavender is very forgiving. You may want to try both methods and see which works best for you.

SPRING PRUNING

In April or May, depending on your zone, cut the plant back one third. You must wait until you see new green growth. This pruning will encourage new growth and help maintain the plant's size. By fall there will be plenty of new leaf cover to protect it from winter damage. After flowering, remove each flower stalk to its base.

SUMMER PRUNING

In April or May check your plants and remove any dead growth. Some gentle shaping is done now. After the first flowers have finished, cut the plant back one third. This usually does not affect the second bloom, but there may not be as much leaf cover for winter protection.

6

LAVENDER PESTS

Lavender is bothered by very few pests. As a result, no pesticides I have seen are licensed for use on lavender. Lavender can be affected by viruses, although in our climate and for the average gardener they do not seem to be a problem.

WHITE FLY *(Trialeurodes vaporariorum)*
Their name is a perfect description. They are small but noticeable little white flying insects, that tend to live on the underside of leaves. These hungry creatures suck liquid from plants at all stages of their development. They also excrete a sticky sap which attracts other insects to the plants. They are more noticeable on plants taken indoors for the winter and can be very hard to get rid of. There are several avenues you can take.

1. Rinse the plant under running water, washing each side of the leaves. You will need to do this every five days to remove this pest during different stages of the life

cycle. If you don't have many, this usually works well.

2. White fly traps. These are bright yellow, sticky strips that attract and catch the flies.

3. Insecticidal soaps. Check your local nursery for advice on products and use.

4. Biological controls. These are not usually necessary for home use, but it is possible to purchase other insects which kill white flies. Check your local nursery for advice.

SPITTLE BUGS *(Philaenus spumarius)*

For evidence of these creatures, look for a wet frothy bubble on the stem. Clear away the froth and you will see a little bright green bug which creates the froth as it chews. In this stage of development they suck fluid from the plants. They are easily knocked off and killed either by hand or with a strong blast of water from the hose. Insecticides are not effective, as the bugs are protected by their frothy cover. Their damage is often minimal.

APHIDS

Often lavender is suggested as a plant that will deter aphids from your garden, yet I have seen aphids on my lavender. These are small green-bodied insects that suck juice from the plant. Like white flies, they secrete a sticky liquid which can in turn cause problems. Aphids are also a concern because they transport plant viruses. They prefer newer growth, and are therefore found near the tips of plants and on buds. They can be easily squashed with your fingers and ladybugs enjoy a good aphid snack. Thanks to my gardening friends, I have learned not to panic at the first sight of aphids.

As I don't use insecticides in the garden, I have a mix of good and bad bugs. Aphids which I see in the morning are usually gone by the afternoon. Insecticidal soaps are effective, but please note—you MUST spray the aphid directly for the soap to work, and you risk harming beneficial insects if you are not careful. Please check with your local nursery for advice if aphids are a problem.

7

LAVENDER IN CONTAINERS

There are many tempting tender varieties. Grow them in pots outside in the summer and enjoy them indoors in the winter. Good drainage is important and can be achieved by making sure the pot has a hole in the bottom, and adding some sand or horticulture grit to the soil. Clay pots give better soil aeration than plastic pots. If your plants will be on a hot, dry patio, the choice of pot really doesn't matter. Check them daily and water thoroughly when the soil is dry to the touch.

Lavender does not like having its roots crowded and may need moving to a larger pot annually. Repotting provides the plants with fresh soil and will probably mean you won't need to fertilize. Otherwise, a little slow-release fertilizer can be added each spring. In the fall, bring the tender plants indoors any time the temperature drops near freezing (0C or 32F). Place them in a bright, south-facing window if you are hoping for winter blooms. I have wintered lavenders in a north window. Water when they are dry. No feeding is needed. In the spring, once the weather is above freezing, your plants can begin the transition outdoors. They will not be used to full sun and will need a sheltered spot with filtered sun at first. Gradually increase the plants' exposure to sunlight and bring them in each night the temperature approaches freezing.

One nursery told me they winter their unsold *L. angustifolia* plants in gallon containers above ground in winter. The nursery is in Zone 6b. This would indicate *L. angustifolia* would be a wonderful container plant that could be left out year-round on a balcony or patio. Containers also give you the option of moving plants around in the garden and filling in bare spots as plants finish blooming. Some, like *Lavandula dentata*, are a nice addition to a mixed planter of other sun-loving annuals. Try it in a container with Gerbera daisies, ivy and *portulaca* for a full-sun location. If you want to bring the *L. dentata* in during the winter, you could put it, pot and all, into the container with the other plants. In the fall, simply remove it from the larger planter and it is ready to go in the house.

L. 'Goodwin Creek Grey' has grey-green woolly foliage that looks lovely in a planter with petunias, heliotrope, and trailing potato vine. The heliotrope and lavender bear purple flowers. By choosing purple petunias and the dark purple potato vine, you will have a sun-loving container with a purple theme. For contrast, select pink or yellow petunias or a variegated potato vine.

HERB CONTAINERS

Lavender will grow well with any of its *Lamiacea* cousins; rosemary, thyme, basil and sage. All these plants have strongly-scented foliage, and to enjoy each fully I would limit my selection to two or three. Try *L. angustifolia* with some of the smaller-leaved creeping thymes. There is a lavender-scented thyme, *Thymus thracicus,* that would be an interesting companion. Group your favourite herbs in a large container with easy access. Add fresh lavender flowers to tea, lemonade, or salad.

LAVENDER TOPIARY

Some varieties of lavender lend themselves to training as topiaries, or standards. Most, unfortunately, are not frost hardy and will need to be brought indoors. Outdoors, place their container into a larger planter and under-plant with sun-loving annuals. Heliotrope, trailing petunias and small marigolds are a few suggestions. Please see the appendix for instructions on making a lavender topiary.

LAVENDER AND BEES

If bees make you nervous, I would suggest you not have more than one or two plants. Bees love lavender and will visit the flowers all day long. If you keep bees for honey, lavender will make a wonderful addition to the plants your bees collect from.

8

Harvesting Lavender

People are usually surprised to learn that for potpourri or culinary use you should harvest lavender flowers in the bud stage. Check your plants each day, and when the first flowers on the stalk open, the stalk is ready to cut. At this time, the buds will be at their best colour and highest oil content.

Try to harvest mid to late morning for the best scent and colour. Do not harvest when the flowers are wet or dew-covered. Wet plant material will not dry well and if the day is overcast, the oil content in the buds will not be as high and the buds not as scented. By late afternoon most of the oils will have evaporated. Harvest the entire stalk by cutting it off where it joins the leafy growth. Tie the lavender in a bunch and hang to dry. Avoid direct sun, as the flowers will fade. Securing the bunch in a paper bag will help the lavender retain its colour. If you are saving the buds, once they are dry simply strip them from the stalks with your fingers and store them in a plastic bag or glass jar out of the sun. The stalks can be put in the fire, on the barbeque, or tied with ribbon and tucked into a drawer. Lavender may also be dried in silica gel, although it will not retain its scent. Lavender flowers may also be pressed.

LAVENDER AND MOTHS

Almost every article about lavender describes women draping their linens over lavender bushes to scent the fabric and repel moths. A few years ago a prominent herb magazine compared lavender varieties and their moth-repelling abilities. They found camphor-scented *L. stoechas* to be the best in the category. However, in Volume 8, December 1983/January 1984 issue of *Perfume and Flavorist* is an article titled "Bulgarian Lavender and Bulgarian Lavender Oil," by I. Ognyanou. He quotes a 1973 study which says, "Bulgarian lavender oil is also an active agent for control of the clothes-moth. It drives away the matured moths and suppresses the growth of their larvae." Do lavender sachets tucked in drawers keep moths away? I have spoken to people who believe they do and have been told of a woman who operates a wool shop who uses lavender essential oil to keep her wool moth-free.

9

PROPAGATING LAVENDER

SEEDS

Cross-pollination among lavender is very common, and growing lavender from seed will not always produce plants true to the variety. If you have a large area, border, or pathway and colour variations are not a concern, then growing from seed can be an economical choice. You can purchase seed, or harvest seeds from your existing plants.

If you already have some lavender plants in the garden, leave some flower stalks on them to set seed. Weed very carefully next spring and watch for emerging blue-grey plants. Check along cracks in stairs or stone paths as these little treasures pop up in the strangest places. This will not work if you have *L. x intermedia* varieties, as these hybrids of *L. angustifolia* and *L. latifolia* are sterile. Fifty years ago, Joan Schofield of Suffolk, Great Britain was fascinated by alpine plants and as an amateur breeder, produced many successful varieties. She experimented with lavenders and by simply paying attention to the seed set on her plants, pollinated by bees, she produced in her third generation of breeding two lavenders still popular today: *L. angustifolia* 'Miss Muffet' and *L. angustifolia* 'Blue Cushion.'

If you live near a protected area, please be careful when allowing plants to self-seed. You would not want to spoil an ecosystem by allowing a non-native plant to run rampant. Remove flower stalks as soon as they finish blooming.

Many seed catalogues and nurseries sell lavender seeds. Some patience will be required, as most will not bloom in their first year. The exception to this is *L. angustifolia* 'Lady.' This All American winner was bred by the Burpee Seed Company of the United States, to produce flowers in the first year, if started early enough indoors. Simply follow the directions on the package. Most *L. angustifolias* will need a cold treatment before they germinate, and this can be accomplished by putting the seeds in the refrigerator for two to three weeks. Use a sterile commercial potting mix. When the seedlings reach 5 cm (2") they can be transplanted into slightly deeper pots and spaced further apart to encourage growth. At this point, I add one part horticultural sand to 3 parts potting mixture to ensure good drainage. Growth at first can be slow, but once established, picks up. I keep my seedlings in pots through the summer in a sunny, but protected area in the garden. Pots should be checked twice a day to prevent them from drying out. At the end of the summer, I move them into the garden bed that will be their home, while making sure the plants are spaced sufficiently so they will not have to be moved again.

CUTTINGS

You will need:

❑ Softwood rooting hormone powder (optional).

❑ Seed-starting soil mix: I have found using half horticultural sand and half seed-starting mix works well, but many growers have developed their own personal favourites. Most commercial seed-starting mixes contain quite a lot of peat moss. This is great for holding water so the cuttings are always moist but seems to keep the soil a little too wet for lavender.

❏ Container: a seed-starting flat or pot. Try to use one not more than 15 cm (6") deep. The cuttings need to be kept moist, but not wet. Water sitting in the soil at the bottom of a deeper pot will not encourage root development.

❏ Softwood cuttings from your lavender plant: These are the freshest growth and appear in spring. Cuttings can be taken later in the season, but the best results are in the spring.

Take cuttings from your plant in the morning. Trim them to 5–8 cm (2–3"). Dip the ends into rooting hormone powder and then into the soil. Space the cuttings 8 cm (3") apart. Most cuttings benefit from a heated bed, and lavender is no exception. If daily watering and checking of the cuttings is not possible, place the container in a plastic bag. Do not put in direct sun, as you will cook the cuttings. Place the container in a protected spot with filtered sun, and check each week. Roots develop at different rates for different varieties, but in general take three to six weeks. Remove any dead cuttings as soon as possible. Once the cuttings have rooted, remove the container from the bag but keep it in the protected spot while the cuttings develop. If they need more space, transplant them into larger pots, again adding some horticultural sand to the commercial potting soil. No fertilizer is needed, as often it has been added to the commercial potting mixture. Cuttings should be ready to plant in their permanent home in the fall.

NOTE: Many varieties are now protected by Plant Breeder's Rights. Plant breeders put money and years, often decades into their breeding programs to bring us new varieties. They deserve to be rewarded and protected for this. You cannot propagate protected plants without permission from the person or nursery who holds the rights to the plant. Plant protection information is usually supplied on the plant tags. When in doubt, contact your local agriculture department or the grower shown on the plant tag.

10

USING LAVENDER

Lavender flowers are beautiful in the garden. Please, do not feel obligated to do anything with them!

FRESH FLOWERS

Cut a bouquet of lavender flowers.

Pick a few stalks as you get into the car. Put them in the back window where the sun will warm the flowers and release the scent into the car. Put the stalks under the floor mat. Your feet will crush the stems and flowers, releasing the scent as you drive.

IN THE KITCHEN

Lemonade

To a pitcher of water add the juice from a lemon, along with five to ten budded lavender stalks. Leave in the refrigerator overnight. Strain and sweeten to taste. This may also be served with fresh mint leaves.

Chicken or Lamb

A cousin of rosemary, lavender can be substituted for rosemary in many recipes. The flavour is strong, so use sparingly.

Add fresh or dried lavender buds to breadcrumbs for stuffing or coating lamb or chicken.

Use fresh flowers to decorate a serving platter or salad.

Lavender scented sugar

Use 15 ml or 1 tablespoon of dried lavender flowers per 4 cups of fine or caster sugar. Blend together and store in an airtight jar for a month, shaking the jar occasionally. The sugar will absorb oils from the lavender flowers and can be used in baking, tea, or custard.

Lavender ice cream

To 2 cups of milk or cream add 2 cups of dried lavender buds. Simmer for 20 minutes and strain. Using this milk, follow the directions of your ice cream maker.

Lavender scones

To your favourite scone recipe add 1/4 cup dried lavender buds.

White cake

To your favourite cake recipe add 1/2 cup of dried lavender buds.

Lavender tisane

To 2 cups of boiling water add 3 tablespoons of fresh lavender flowers. Steep for 3 to 4 minutes, then strain. Sweeten to taste with honey or sugar, and serve with a slice of lemon. This drink was apparently a favourite of Queen Elizabeth I.

DRIED LAVENDER

Potpourri

Making your dried flowers into scented blends is simple. Ensure your plant material is thoroughly dry. Gum benzoin and orris root powder are two common fixatives. They help potpourri keep its fragrance, but are not necessary. Each have a light scent of their own which will be imparted to the final mix.

Simply lavender

Dried flower buds

Lavender essential oil: use 15 to 20 drops per cup of flowers.

Fixative: use 1/2 teaspoon per cup of dried flowers. This is optional.

In a plastic bag, combine dried lavender flowers, oil and fixative. Shake well. Store out of direct sun for several weeks, shaking occasionally. This spreads the oils and fixative evenly throughout the blend.

Simple sachets

The simplest sachets can be make with lacy handkerchiefs. Place a handful of potpourri in the centre of the handkerchief. Gather the cloth around the potpourri and tie closed with a ribbon.

Relaxing potpourri blend

1 cup dried lemon verbena

1 cup dried rose petals

1 cup dried chamomile flowers

2 cups dried lavender flowers

60 drops of lavender essential oil

(1 cup of dried hops flowers. This is optional. Hops have a lovely grassy scent but they do not appeal to everyone.)

In a plastic bag combine ingredients. Shake well. Store out of direct sun for several weeks, shaking occasionally.

Lavender-flax eye bags
1/2 cup dried lavender buds
1/2 cup flax seed

There are several easy ways to make these. One uses a clean, soft sock. Fill it with your lavender-flax mixture. Sew the opening closed, or tie closed with a ribbon. Another way is also very simple to sew. You will need a 20 cm by 20 cm (8" by 8") square of fabric. Satin is cool and soft, but cotton also works well. Fold the right sides of the fabric together and stitch three sides closed. Turn inside out. Fill with lavender-flax mixture and sew the remaining side closed.

Popular as gifts, these are used simply by placing the soft bag across your eyes. The lavender helps with relaxation while the flax seed gives an acupressure treatment to your eyelids. They can be kept in the freezer to use cold or gently heated in the microwave to use warm. Heat slowly as you do not want to cook the flax seed.

11

LAVENDER ESSENTIAL OIL

WHAT ARE ESSENTIAL OILS?

Crush a mint leaf between your fingers and inhale the refreshing odour. You are inhaling a certain combination of chemicals. Crush a lavender leaf or flower and you are treated to a different scent; a different combination of naturally occurring chemicals. When these chemicals are removed from the plant they are highly concentrated and are known as *essential oils*. Lavender essential oil contains over one hundred known chemicals. They evaporate easily, explaining why you can smell lavender by simply brushing against a plant.

Browse any book on aromatherapy and see the large number of plants that produce essential oils: mints for candies and mouthwashes; rose petals for perfumes and oils; chamomile for pharmaceutical ointments, hair and bath products; pine oil (from pine trees) for soaps, detergents, and toiletries. Thousands of years ago, someone discovered these oils could be extracted from flowers, barks, and leaves. One of the early methods was to put the plant material in a piece of cloth, place it into oil and leave it for a prescribed amount of time. The scented chemicals leached from the plant material into the oil. There were a selection of base oils from which to choose: castor, linseed, sesame, safflower, almond, and olive. Occasionally the plant material was boiled in a mixture of water and base oil. When cool, the base oil, now infused with essential oil, floated to the top and was skimmed off.

Essential oils were originally used for ointments and perfumes. From ancient times, preparing perfumes required great skill. The plants and spices, nearly all of which were imported, were very expensive. Growers and perfumers organised into family-based guilds to protect their secrets and profits.

Today lavender essential oil is produced by steam distillation. Lavender flowers, with attached leaves and stalks, are packed into large metal vats. Steam is pushed through the material, rupturing the plant cells. The intense heat causes the plant oils to become vapour. They blend with the steam and are carried through tubing to a large glass jar. As the blend of steam and vapour cools, it becomes oil and water. The oil, being lighter in weight, rests on top of the water and is siphoned off. The remaining water is infused with lavender oil and called a *hydrolate* or *hydrosol*. This water is used by aromatherapists, or occasionally in cooking, where only a hint of flavour is needed.

Large amounts of plant material are needed to produce even a small amount of oil. While yields vary, on average it requires 5 kilos (11 pounds) of lavender to produce 15 millilitres of essential oil. A 15-millilitre bottle is approximately 6 cm (2.5") in height. That is quite a good return, and as a result lavender essential oil is reasonably priced.

The term *aromatherapy* began when French chemist Dr. Ren-Maurice Gattfoss titled his 1937 book *Aromatherapy*. It refers to the use of essential oils. To check the quality of an oil, put a few drops on a white piece of paper. A good quality oil will completely evaporate, leaving no residue.

TYPES OF LAVENDER ESSENTIAL OILS

There are many varieties of lavenders and it is not surprising there are variations in lavender essential oils. The oil name usually reflects the variety of the plant the oil came from. Another term you may hear is *therapeutic grade essential oil*. These oils are used by aromatherapists, where quality is paramount. There are many excellent quality oils available for home use.

Among the more common are

L. angustifolia: this is only from *L. angustifolia* plants. The scent may vary slightly, depending on where the oil originated.

L. officinalis: In general, this is the oil we associate with the scent of lavender. Often it is from *L. angustifolia* plants, but it may be Lavender 40/42. It is suitable for home use.

Lavender 40/42: This is sometimes sold as *L. officinalis*. The *40* represents the linalool content, while the *42* represents the linalyl acetate content. They are the predominant naturally-occurring chemicals in lavender. As the quality of lavender oil may change from year to year, Lavender 40/42 was developed in France as a standardised product. New lavender oil was tested (using gas chromatography) and, if necessary, supplemented with these natural chemicals. It is widely available, has a classic lavender fragrance, and is suitable for home use.

The following oils are occasionally available. Their scents are sharper than L. officinalis.

L. grosso: May also be called *Lavandin Grosso*.

L. dentata: May also be called French lavender.

L. latifolia: May also be called spike lavender. It has a strong camphor odour and would only be used by a professional.

L. stoechas: Not often available. It has a high ketone content and could be potentially toxic. Use only with a professional.

PRODUCING YOUR OWN LAVENDER OIL

Distilling lavender oil is not practical for most of us. First you need distilling equipment. Then you need quite a bit of plant material to produce a small amount of oil. Many essential oil producers routinely have their oils checked by laboratories to ensure the uniformity and quality of their product. That said, home distilling equipment is available for those who want to produce their own. To find suppliers, look in herb magazines and on the internet. A search of *distil lavender* brought up several manufacturers.

SIMPLE SCENTED OIL

Following ancient traditions, pack lavender leaves and flowers into a jar and cover with a base oil: sweet almond oil, jojoba oil, olive oil, castor oil, etc. Cover the jar and let sit in full sun for two weeks, then strain. The base oil will now be infused with some of the lavender's essential oils for a delicate scent. This oil can be used as a massage oil, or used in the bath, either on its own or blended with Epsom salts.

USING LAVENDER ESSENTIAL OIL

Lavender essential oil is used in perfumes, soaps, lotion, insect repellents, room sprays; for skin problems, and for treating burns. It is among the safest of essential oils to use. Many people find lavender helps them relax and sleep. Lavender has been shown to be mood-balancing. It will help you relax if you are stressed, may lift you if you are depressed, and a minority of people find it makes them hyperactive. Recently studies on the calming effect of lavender have been done with people suffering from dementias. One study in Australia followed 56 patients with different dementias in a seniors' facility. Patients were gently stroked with a cream containing lavender, sweet marjoram, patchouli and *vetivert* essential oils five times a day for four weeks. The same cream, without essential oils, was used for an additional four weeks. The patients' behaviour was recorded throughout the eight-week study. The results showed that not only were the patients calmer, but the staff themselves reported a greater sense of well-being with the scented cream.[2]

IN THE BEDROOM

Try 1–3 drops of lavender oil near your pillow each night for a restful sleep. As essential oils may stain a pillowcase, try placing a few drops on a tissue near your pillow.
Place a small bowl of dried lavender flowers near your bed. Each night add a few drops of oil.

IN THE BATH

Add 5–10 drops to a warm bath just as you are ready to get in. Lavender bath salts are easily made by blending sea salts or Epsom salts with lavender essential oil. Per cup of salts use 10–15 drops of oil. Mix thoroughly. Use half a cup of mixture per bath. Use immediately or store in a plastic bag or glass jar to keep the oil from evaporating.

---

[2] Dr. Heather Cavanagh. "Recent Developments in the Science of Lavender. Conference Abstracts." *The Lavender Bag*, November 2001, p. 7.

LOTIONS

A variety of books are available showing how to make creams and lotions from scratch. A simple lavender lotion can be made using a quality unscented hand or body lotion and adding lavender essential oil to it. Use 1–2 drops of oil per tablespoon of lotion. Blend together and use immediately.

LAUNDRY

Add 5–10 drops to a load of laundry for a refreshing scent. The laundry room will smell nice as well! Place 5–10 drops on an old facecloth and put in the dryer to scent clothes while they dry.

SCENTING A ROOM

People often comment that after they have been in a room for a while they don't notice the scent. Before you increase the scent, leave the room for a few minutes and re-enter. You may be surprised how fragrant the room really is.

SCENT BURNER

This is a popular method for room fragrance. Essential oils will evaporate without the use of a candle; however, the gentle heat speeds the process while adding atmosphere to the room. Do not leave the candle unattended.

HUMIDIFIER

Add a few drops of lavender oil to the humidifier.

ROOM SPRAY

This is my favourite way to scent a room. There is no candle to watch and different oils are easily blended together for unique combinations. The scent is made as strong or weak as needed by varying the amount of oil I use. Per cup of distilled water, use 8–10 drops of oil. Put into a spray bottle, shake well before use and spray into the air. Distilled water is preferred, as chemicals in regular water will affect the lavender oil.

SAFETY NOTES

Information given here is not intended to replace medical advice.

Essential oils are very strong and should not be used directly on the skin without diluting first with a base oil: sweet almond oil, jojoba oil, olive oil, castor oil, etc.

Essential oils will damage paint and varnish finishes on furniture, so use carefully. It only takes a few drops to damage the finish on furniture. Essential oils are not soluble in water. If you spill any on furniture, try using a base oil (as listed above) on a cloth to wipe the area first. This will dilute and help remove the essential oil. The area can then be cleaned with a little soap and water.

Essential oils will burn mucous membranes in nose and eyes. Keep oils away from your eyes. If you get any in your eyes, flush immediately with water and contact a health practitioner.

Lavender essential oil contains chemicals which help cell growth. Never use lavender oil on a puncture wound as it may close over too quickly. Puncture wounds should heal from the inside out.

Children and babies have a very sensitive sense of smell. One or two drops is usually plenty. The fact that you cannot detect the scent does not mean a child cannot.

Essential oils are highly concentrated. A few drops go a long way.

Essential oil quality is affected by ultraviolet light and oils should be stored in brown glass. Exposure to air will also affect quality. Once the bottle is opened it should be used within the year.

Essential oils do not always mix with homeopathy. Check with your health practitioner before using essential oils.

12

Lavender Varieties

Plant names

Most plants have three names: the variety name, the botanical name and the common name. The common name is the name most people recognise a plant by, such as petunia, zinnia, sunflower, or lavender. Common names for lavender include English lavender, Dutch lavender and French lavender. Here is the problem—French lavender can refer to any number of varieties or the country of origin. Common names tend to change regionally, so one plant may have several common names, causing confusion. The pretty annual flower *Centaurea cyanus*, has several common names in Southern Ontario: bachelor buttons and corn-flower. At a presentation I gave on growing lavender, a woman asked why her sea lavender plant didn't resemble any of the lavender plants I had brought with me. Sea lavender is *Statice caroliniana*, part of the *Statice* genus, and not a lavender at all. As lavender may also refer to a plant colour, the confusion easily multiplies.

Botanists developed the idea of giving plants

standard names. These are called botanical names. Botanical names have two parts. The first name refers to the genus the plant belongs to. All members of the lavender genus begin their botanical name with *Lavandula*. It is sometimes shown simply as a capital *L*. For example, *Lavandula angustifolia* may be shown as *L. angustifolia*.

The second part is the species name. Within the *Lavandula* genus are thirty-two to thirty-six species, each with unique characteristics. The species name is shown in italics and is not capitalized. We'll use our example of *Lavandula angustifolia*. Examples of two other species are *L. lanata* and *L. latifolia*. All the plants within a species are related, but may differ in size or colour. These are called varieties or cultivars. Their names are shown in inverted comas. *L. angustifolia* 'Hidcote' and *L. angustifolia* 'Munstead' are both different varieties of the same species.

The following is by no means a complete list of lavenders available, but the most common in this area. Understanding the names and potential uses will help you select other lavenders your local nursery may offer. Under the botanical names appear any common names these plants are known by. When shopping for lavender, I suggest you write down both botanical and common names and take them with you. (Author's note: *Lavender. The Growers Guide* offers a complete study of lavender varieties. See bibliography for details.)

Height refers to mature plants, which are usually three to four years old. A lavender bud is called a *calyx*. The flower is called the *corolla*. The bud colour is listed separately from the flower colour for two reasons. If you are drying lavender for potpourri, it is the bud you will be collecting. In some cases, the bud colour will help identify the plants.

LAVANDULA ANGUSTIFOLIA

These are also known as English lavenders.

One of the largest lavender species, it contains the most winter-hardy and colourful varieties. Some are small enough for the rock garden, others large enough to make a statement! The earliest lavenders to bloom in the garden, most will bloom in June or July and again in August and September.

Lavandula angustifolia
(L. vera, L. officinalis, true lavender, *L. spica,*
Dutch lavender, English lavender)

Plant height:	45 cm (18")
Flowering height:	60 cm (24")
Bud colour:	lavender-green
Flower colour:	light blue-violet
Zone hardiness:	5, but possibly further north.

Uses: Cut flower, rock garden, garden flower, herb garden, edging paths, containers, essential oil, culinary.

Here is a plant with the same name as the species! It differs from *L. angustifolia* 'Hidcote' in that the flowers are paler and the flower spike has a break between the groups of flowers. Readily available at garden centres, this fragrant lavender is a versatile addition to any garden. A well-maintained and pruned plant may live twenty years. On a garden tour one summer, the hostess indicated a blooming lavender plant that was in the garden when they bought the house thirty years ago.

Native to the Pyrenees in southern France, Switzerland, north-east Spain and northern Italy, this is believed to be one of the original sources of lavender essential oil; the lavender the French collected in the mountains and carried to the valley stills. Eventually, hybrids of *L. angustifolia* and *L. latifolia* produced larger plants, more flowers, and more oil per acre, and *L. angustifolia* was replaced. It is still possible to purchase lavender essential oil extracted only from *L. angustifolia* plants, as they continue to be grown in Bulgaria, Croatia, France, Australia, England and Jersey Island. Oil from *L. angustifolia* should be so indicated on the label.

Lavandula angustifolia 'Munstead'
('Munstead Blue,' 'Munstead Dwarf')

Plant height:	30–40 cm (12–16")
Flowering height:	40–50 cm (16–20")
Bud colour:	violet-blue
Flower colour:	lavender-blue
Zone hardiness:	5, but possibly zone 2 with protection.

Uses: Cut flower, dried buds, rock gardens, garden flower, herb garden, edging paths, culinary.

'Munstead' is the most winter hardy of all the lavenders. Although shown here as winter hardy to zone 5, I heard from a woman who winters it in her zone 2 garden with protection. A wonderful garden plant grown since the early 1900s, it is at home in the herb garden or rock garden. Commonly grown from seed, it may have some variation from original type. Still it remains a staple lavender for the northern gardener. The flowers tend to appear bunched in a group about 3 cm (1") long at the top of the flower spike. Its colour is lighter than *L. angustifolia* 'Hidcote.'

Lavandula angustifolia 'Hidcote'
('Hidcote Blue,' 'Hidcote Purple')

Plant height: 60–70 cm (24–28")
Flowering height: 70–80 cm (28–32")
Bud colour: dark violet
Flower colour: violet
Zone hardiness: 5, but possibly zone 4.

Uses: Hedge, garden, rock garden, cut flower, dried buds, dried buds on the stalk, essential oil, culinary.

A beautiful, fragrant plant which reliably blooms twice a season. The flower spikes, in colour and form, are what we traditionally think of as lavender. They hold their colour and scent well when dried. The dried buds hold to the stalk if you are looking for lavender stalks for craft projects. Like 'Munstead,' 'Hidcote' has been grown from seed in the past and some colour variation may exist among plants if you purchase them from different sources. It is believed to have been raised by Major Lawrence Johnston at Hidcote Manor in Great Britain, around 1950.

Lavandula angustifolia 'Lady'
('Lavender Lady')

Plant height: 40–50 cm (16–20")
Flowering height: 50–60 cm (20–24")
Bud colour: violet
Flower colour: violet-blue
Zone hardiness: 5

Uses: Garden, rock garden, cut flower, dried buds, culinary.

This lovely lavender is one of the newest on the market and in 1994 was an All American Selection winner. It was bred by W. Atlee Burpee and Company of the United States. Using *L. angustifolia* 'Munstead,' they bred the plants until they produced lavender that would grow true to type from seed and bloom in the first year. This was quite an achievement, as most lavenders, whether started as cuttings or from seed, bloom in the second year. To achieve bloom in the first year, you need to start the seed indoors in January or February. This means it can be grown as an annual in colder zones. It benefits from pruning to keep its size and shape.

Lavandula angustifolia 'Jean Davis'

Plant height:	60–70 cm (24–28")
Flowering height:	70–80 cm (28–32")
Bud colour:	green with a hint of red-purple
Flower colour:	soft lavender-pink
Zone hardiness:	5

Uses: Hedges, cut flowers, garden flower, rock garden.

In my area, there are two pink varieties available. They are *L. angustifolia* 'Jean Davis' and *L. angustifolia* 'Rosea.' They are similar in size and growth habit. However, the actual flowering spike of *L. angustifolia* 'Rosea' is longer and the colour a deeper pink, giving more contrast in the garden. In some cases, the names of these plants have been interchanged so acquiring an actual *L. angustifolia* 'Jean Davis' may not be possible.

Lavandula angustifolia 'Rosea'

Plant height:	60–70 cm (24–28")
Flowering height:	75–90 cm (30–35")
Bud colour:	green with a hint of red-purple
Flower colour:	mauve-pink
Zone hardiness:	5

Uses: Hedges, cut flowers, garden flower, rock garden, dried flowers.

See *Lavandula angustifolia* 'Jean Davis' above.

This beautiful pink lavender has been grown since 1937. The pretty pink provides a lovely contrast in the garden when planted with darker varieties. The dried bunches are very pale.

Lavandula angustifolia 'Nana Alba'
('Dwarf White,' 'Baby White')

Plant height:	30–40 cm (12–16")
Flowering height:	36–50 cm (14–20")
Bud colour:	green
Flower colour:	white
Zone hardiness:	5

Uses: Cut flowers, garden flower, rock garden, garden paths.

This beautiful white variety shows compact growth. It is pretty in bloom or not, making it ideal for a small garden. It was introduced prior to 1938. There is another *L. angustifolia* with the name 'Nana.' It is a purple-flowering variety and should not be confused with 'Nana Alba.'

Lavandula angustifolia 'Twickle Purple'

Plant height:	60–70 cm (24–28")
Flowering height:	86–100 cm (34–40")
Bud colour:	violet-green
Flower colour:	deep violet
Zone hardiness:	5

Uses: Cut flowers, garden flower, dried buds, lavender wands.

Long spikes holding violet flowers make this plant stunning in the garden. A large plant, it requires space to do it justice. Regular spring pruning is required to keep its shape.

Lavandula angustifolia 'Blue Cushion'

Plant height: 30 cm (12")
Flowering height: 60 cm (24")
Bud colour: green with violet-blue
Flower colour: bright violet-blue
Zone hardiness: 5; maybe zone 4

Uses: Cut flowers, garden flower, rock garden, borders, dried buds, low hedge.

This charming dwarf plant with grey-green foliage flowers freely all season. It was introduced in 1992.

Lavandula angustifolia 'Cynthia Johnson'

Plant height: 30 cm (12")
Flowering height: 60 cm (24")
Bud colour: lavender
Flower colour: violet-purple
Zone hardiness: 3

Uses: Cut flowers, garden flower, rock garden, small hedge.

This is a fairly new variety, with attractive silver-green foliage, that is hardy to zone 3.

LAVANDULA LATIFOLIA

Lavandula latifolia
('Spike Lavender')

Plant height: 40 cm (16")
Flowering height: 100 cm (40")
Bud colour: grey-violet
Flower colour: mauve-violet
Zone hardiness: 9

Uses: Specimen plant

L. latifolia is not winter hardy. Often the flower spikes are branched and carry multiple flowers stalks. *L. latifolia*, sometimes called *Lavandula spica,* or 'spike lavender,' was used to produce an essential oil used in soaps, disinfectants and varnish. It tends to be disease-prone and is not as tolerant of damp conditions as other lavenders. It hybridizes easily with *L. angustifolias* and the real value of this plant has been its offspring, the *Lavandula x intermedia* family, which have become the backbone of the lavender oil industry.

LAVANDULA X INTERMEDIA
(Sometimes called 'lavandins')

This species is a natural hybrid of *L. angustifolia* and *L. latifolia,* and unfortunately, all are sterile. Colours are primarily shades of violets and purples although there are a few white varieties. *Lavandula x intermedia* hybrids have several members which are winter hardy to zone 5. While their essential oil may not be as nicely scented as *L. angustifolia*, the yield of oil can be five times that of *L. angustifolia.* They tend to bloom several weeks later than *L. angustifolias* and often bloom twice in the season. Many of these varieties are bred so the dried buds fall easily from the stems. This makes collecting dried buds simple, but if you are looking for stalks that will stay intact when dry, stay with the *L. angustifolias.* This group has over 20 varieties. Only a few are mentioned here.

L x intermedia 'Abrialii'

Plant height:	70 cm (28")
Flowering height:	100 cm (40")
Bud colour:	violet-blue

Flower colour: violet-blue
Zone hardiness: 5

Uses: Cut flowers, garden flower, ornamental plant, lavender wands. dried buds, essential oil. This is a large beautiful lavender for your garden.

Lavandula x intermedia 'Goldburg'
(*L. angustifolia* 'Goldburg')

Plant height: 30–40 cm (12–16")
Flowering height: 40–47 cm (16–18")
Bud colour: lavender
Flower colour: deep lavender-blue
Zone hardiness: 5 or 6

Uses: Cut flowers, garden flower, rock garden, garden paths.

This variety has unique variegated leaves which are green, edged in a creamy yellow. The flowers are a beautiful deep colour and the plant has a lovely scent. This is a newer variety and already some of the information available is contradictory. Several places have this listed as *L x intermedia* (a hybrid of *L. angustifolia* and *L. latifolia*), while the breeder in the Netherlands registered it as *L. angustifolia*. 'Goldburg' is supposed to be winter hardy to zone 5a; however, gardeners in my zone 5 area have had trouble wintering it. I had it survive the first winter. We had a very mild spell in March and it was still alive. This mild weather was followed by a lot of rain, and by May my plant had died. This leads me to suspect that good drainage is paramount for its success. It is a stunning plant in bloom.

Lavandula x intermedia 'Grosso'

Plant height: 70 cm (28")
Flowering height: 100 cm (40")
Bud colour: violet
Flower colour: violet-blue
Zone hardiness: 5

Uses: Cut flowers, garden flower, border flower, ornamental plant, lavender wands, dried buds, essential oil.

If you have room for a large lavender, this plant is beautiful, in and out of bloom. 'Grosso' was discovered in France in 1972. At the time, *L x intermedia* 'Abrialii' was commonly grown for oil, and being affected by disease. Someone noticed how healthy the 'Grosso' plants were, and gradually it became the popular commercial variety.

Lavandula x intermedia 'Hidcote Giant'

Plant height: 80 cm (31")
Flowering height: 110 cm (44")
Bud colour: deep violet-blue
Flower colour: violet-blue
Zone hardiness: 5

Uses: Cut flowers, garden flower, dried buds, lavender wands.

Lovely grey-green foliage on a large plant. The flower heads are a medium length, but packed tight with flowers.

Lavandula x intermedia 'Provence'

Plant height: 45–60 cm (18–24")
Flowering height: 91 cm (36")
Bud colour: green with violet
Flower colour: dark violet
Zone hardiness: 5

Uses: Cut flowers, garden flower, culinary, dried buds, lavender wands.

This is a lovely garden lavender. It requires more space than *L. angustifolia* 'Hidcote,' but not as much room as *L. x intermedia* 'Grosso.' This plant was bred in the United States. It is not recommended for essential oil production.

Lavandula x intermedia 'Seal'

Plant height:	45–60 cm (18–24")
Flowering height:	91 cm (36")
Bud colour:	green with violet
Flower colour:	bright violet-blue
Zone hardiness:	5

Uses: Cut flowers, garden flower, ornamental plant, dried buds, lavender wands.

The first time I visited lavender farms, at each place I was drawn to a large, bloom-covered plant ,and in every instance the plant was *L. x intermedia* 'Seal.' Its flower buds are supposed to retain their scent for a long time, making this an excellent choice for sachets and potpourris. This variety dates from at least 1935 and was raised at the Herb Farm in Seal, Great Britain.

Lavandula x intermedia 'Walberton's Silver Edge'
(*L. angustifolia* 'Silver Edge,' *Lavandula x intermedia* 'Silver Edge')

Plant height:	40 cm (16")
Flowering height:	60 cm (24")
Bud colour:	soft green with blue-violet
Flower colour:	light lavender-blue
Zone hardiness:	5

Uses: Cut flowers, garden flower, rock garden, containers.

Attractive grey-green foliage edged in creamy yellow gives this lavender a light feathery appearance. The foliage is sweetly scented and provides a lovely contrast to other garden lavenders. Introduced in 1999, it is sold as *L. angustifolia* and as *L x intermedia*. The *L. x intermedia* classification comes from the Royal Horticultural Society. This lavender was originally grown at Walberton Nursery in West Sussex, Great Britain.

David Tristram of Walberton Nursery told me 'Silver Edge' originated from a seedling of a plant named *L. vera*, which they believed to be *L. angustifolia*. Occasionally a plant will spontaneously mutate and produce a plant with a different colour foliage or flower. This happens in roses and it happened with this seedling. Where there were broad green leaves, there were suddenly variegated leaves. They worked with these until able to produce plants with stable colouring. *L. x. intermedia* are hybrids between *L. angustifolia* and *L. latifolia*, and 'Silver Edge' could certainly be one. They know one parent was *L. angustifolia*. These hybrids are sterile, and if 'Silver Edge' is sterile, the classification will eventually be confirmed. Simply be aware that this pretty plant may appear under either species.

TENDER LAVENDER VARIETIES

There are some wonderful lavenders, not frost hardy, well worth growing as potted plants. Plant them in containers with other annuals for texture and colour. Grow them as annuals or bring them into the house or greenhouse to over-winter, taking them outside again when the danger of frost is past. The heights given for these plants refer to growing them in the ground. You would need to grow them in large containers for them to achieve their maximum size.

LAVANDULA STOECHAS
('Spanish lavender')

Off the Mediterranean coast of France is a group of islands once called the Stoechades by the Greeks, and from which this group of lavenders derives its name. The flower heads are characterized by what look like extra petals on top of the flower head. Sometimes called *rabbit ears* or *wings*, their correct name is *sterile bracts*. These plants bloom throughout the summer. The foliage of *L. stoechas* has a camphor scent. They are gaining popularity as potted plants and are often outside restaurants in downtown Toronto, and are available at florists. They come in a variety of colours, and the following are just a few varieties available.

Lavandula stoechas subspecies stoechas
('Italian lavender,' 'French lavender,' 'Spanish lavender')

Plant height:	46 cm (18")
Flowering height:	54 cm (21")
Bud colour:	purple
Flower colour:	dark purple
Zone hardiness:	8–10

Uses: Container plant, garden plant.

Lovely purple bracts crown this pretty plant. Native to the Mediterranean area, including North Africa, Portugal and Madeira.

Lavandula stoechas 'Fairy Wings'

Plant height:	48 cm (19")
Flowering height:	61 cm (24")
Bud colour:	plum

Flower colour: plum
Zone hardiness: 7

Uses: Cut flowers, container plant, garden plant.

A new introduction, with long lilac-pink sterile bracts which make quite a contrast to the darker flower heads.

Lavandula stoechas 'Hazel'

Plant height: 61 cm (24")
Flowering height: 76 cm (30")
Bud colour: violet
Flower colour: deep violet
Zone hardiness: 8

Uses: Cut flowers, container plant, garden plant.

This is a newer variety from Invercargill, New Zealand, and is named after Australian Hazel Tildsey. The flowers and sterile bracts are a beautiful dark violet colour, making it a striking plant.

Lavandula stoechas 'Marshwood'

Plant height: 90 cm (36")
Flowering height: 110 cm (42")
Bud colour: green with red-purple
Flower colour: deep blue
Zone hardiness: 8–10

Uses: Cut flowers, container plant, garden plant.

Brilliant pink-violet sterile bracts resemble butterflies dancing on a breeze on this striking plant. Raised in New Zealand by Geoff and Adair Grange in the late 1980s, it remains popular today.

Lavandula stoechas subspecies. pedunculata
('French lavender peduncled,' *L. pedunculata*, 'Spanish lavender')

Plant height:	75 cm (30")
Flowering height:	90 cm (35")
Bud colour:	green with red-purple tinge to tip
Flower colour:	dark blue
Zone hardiness:	8–10

Uses: Cut flowers, container plant, garden plant.

Long flower stalks, purple flowers and lovely purple sterile bracts make this an elegant plant. Leaves are narrow, a pale grey-green and camphor scented. The name *pedunculata* refers to the particularly long stalk which carries the flowers. One source indicates this lavender may survive to -5C. This plant is found in a number of countries, including the Atlantic islands, Spain, Portugal, North Africa and Asia Minor.

Lavandula viridis

Plant height:	70–100cm (28–40")
Flowering height:	80–115 cm (32–46")
Bud colour:	green
Flower colour:	white-green
Zone hardiness:	9

The name *viridis* refers to this plant's green colour. It is a pretty plant with bright green foliage. A green tinge appears in the flowers and sterile bracts. Classification of this plant has changed recently. Sometimes it is given its own classification and sometimes it is listed with *L. stoechas* varieties. I managed to find some seeds for sale and decided to give them a try. They germinated in the house and were transplanted into pots and put on the patio for the summer. They grew well; however, they did not tolerate the move into the house for the winter. Many lavenders will tolerate mild drought conditions in the house and recover well when watered thoroughly. The *L. viridis* plants did not tolerate their pots being really dry, and once wilting started it was hard for them to recover. This unique lavender is worth the extra attention. It is native to south-west Spain, southern Portugal and Madeira.

OTHER LAVENDERS

Lavandula canariensis

Plant height:	60 cm (24")
Flowering height:	100 cm (40")
Bud colour:	green with purple tip
Flower colour:	violet-tinged blue
Zone hardiness:	9

Uses: Container plant.

This is an unusual lavender with lacy, camphor-scented foliage. The woody stems are best pruned in February or March to keep this plant's growth in check. It's adaptable to patio or house.

Lavandula 'Goodwin Creek Grey'

Plant height:	70 cm (28")
Flowering height:	100 cm (40")
Bud colour:	green with violet
Flower colour:	violet
Zone hardiness:	9

Uses: Cut flowers, container plant, topiary.

Beautiful silver-grey woolly foliage makes this is a lovely plant in or out of bloom. It is thought to be an offspring of "woolly" *Lavandula lanata* and perhaps *Lavandula dentata*. The unusual foliage colour and texture mixes well with container plants outdoors in the summer. Indoors in the winter it is problem free, tolerant of dry soil, and occasionally provides January blooms. It was raised at Goodwin Creek Gardens in Oregon, United States.

Lavandula x heterophylla
('Sweet lavender,' *Lavandula heterophylla*)

Plant height:	80 cm (32")
Flowering height:	100 cm (40")
Bud colour:	green with violet
Flower colour:	violet
Zone hardiness:	9

Uses: Cut flowers, container plant, flower wands.

With lovely grey-green indented foliage, this plant has the sweet scent we associate with lavender. It will bloom several times during the year and is a fine container and house plant, giving good growth with minimum care. It is thought to be a hybrid of *L. angustifolia* and *L. dentata* and seems to be sterile.

Lavandula dentata
('French lavender')

Plant height:	45–60 cm (18–24")
Flowering height:	91 (36")
Bud colour:	green with violet
Flower colour:	light blue-violet
Zone hardiness:	9

Uses: Container plant, topiary.

Bright green leaves have a strong camphor-lavender scent. The flower heads are topped with mauve sterile bracts. It is not as frost tolerant as some other *L. dentatas.* A local garden centre was selling it as an annual and it makes a nice addition to containers. It is a vigorous grower and does well in the house.

Lavandula dentata var. candicans
('French Grey,' 'Spanish Grey')

Plant height:	100 cm (40")
Flowering height:	120 cm (48")
Bud colour:	green, tipped violet
Flower colour:	light violet-blue
Zone hardiness:	9

Uses: Cut flowers, topiary, container plant.

This *L. dentata* species has serrated silvery-grey leaves with texture and scent. It has small sterile bracts at the top of the flower head. Its upright growth habit makes it a fine choice for topiaries. Some sources suggest it will tolerate a light frost. It is native to North Africa, Madeira, and the Cape Verde Islands. I have found it adapts nicely indoors in the winter.

Lavandula dentate 'Linda Ligon'

Plant height:	70–80 cm (28–32")
Flowering height:	90 cm (36")
Bud colour:	green with violet
Flower colour:	dark lavender
Zone hardiness:	8

Uses: Topiary, container plant.

'Linda Ligon' has upright growth, making it a good topiary candidate. The bright green foliage is variegated with a creamy-yellow colour. Although the variegation is not as even as *L. x intermedia* 'Goldburg' or 'Silver Edge,' it is an attractive, unusual plant. Some sources suggest it will tolerate a light frost. It was raised in the United States by Tom DeBaggio.

Lavandula lanata
('Woolly lavender')

Plant height:	45 cm (18")
Flowering height:	80 cm (32")
Bud colour:	green with violet, fuzzy texture
Flower colour:	deep violet- purple
Zone hardiness:	8

Uses: Ornamental plant.

Broad woolly leaves characterize this unique lavender. In fact, the entire plant has a texture of velvet. It is native to southern Spain where it grows on dry calcareous hills, and this is the clue to cultivating it. It requires excellent drainage and a higher pH than most other lavenders. If you have one that is struggling, one grower suggests adding lime to the soil. If velvet foliage attracts you, I would recommend *L.* 'Goodwin Creek Gray' instead as it is much easier to grow.

Lavandula multifida
('Fern leaf lavender')

Plant height:	30 cm (12")
Flowering height:	36 cm (14")
Bud colour:	green, hairy
Flower colour:	blue-violet
Zone hardiness:	9

Uses: Ornamental plant.

The leaves are sparsely haired with a light lemon-camphor scent. The stalks have a tendency to be woody. It is a charming plant with delicate, lacy foliage. It is native to the western Mediterranean, Portugal and North Africa.

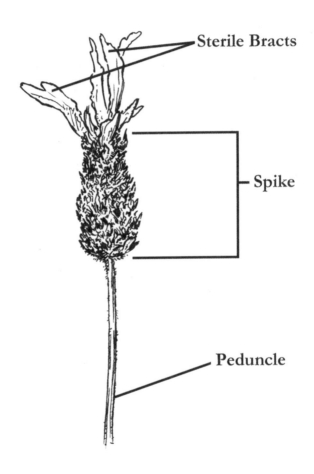

Sterile Bracts

Spike

Peduncle

L. *stoeachas* flower

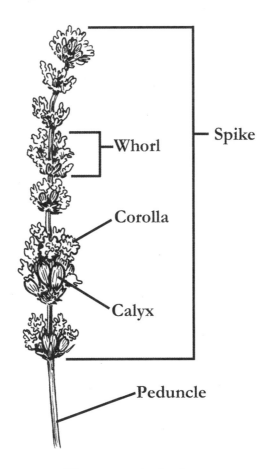

Spike

Whorl

Corolla

Calyx

Peduncle

Flower typical of
L. *angustifolia*, L. x *intermedia*

Large commercial lavender plant

Lavandula canariensis

Pink and white lavender at Norfolk Lavender, England

Lavandula stoechas 'Marshwood'

Norfolk Lavender. Front to back: L. a. 'Miss Katherine'; L. a. 'Backhouse Nana'; L. a. 'Beechwood Blue'; L. a. 'Bowles'; L. a. 'Hidcote'; L. xi. 'Seal' (tall variety at back)

Lavender and roses. Norfolk Lavender

Raised bed near the bus stop in St. Helene, Jersey Island

Lavandula viridis. Jersey Lavender Farm

Appendix 1

MAKING A LAVENDER TOPIARY

Lavender plants have a tendency to develop a woody stem, which makes them ideal candidates for topiaries. Some varieties are better suited than others. *L. x heterophylla, L. dentata, L. dentata var. candicans* and *L.* 'Goodwin Creek Grey' are among the best choices. The *L. angustifolias*, such as *L. angustifolia* 'Hidcote' and *L. angustifolia* 'Munstead' would seem to be ideal for smaller topiaries. However, they have a tendency to grow horizontally rather than vertically, and can be hard to keep properly shaped.

To make a topiary requires patience. Begin with a small plant, about four inches tall. Remove all stems, with the exception of the straightest one. Insert a bamboo stake the height of your eventual topiary into the soil. With a twist-tie, loosely attach the stem to the stake. Some growers remove half of the bottom leaves at this point, while others leave them on until the plant reaches the desired height.

When the stem reaches the height of the bamboo stake, cut off a little of the very top of the stem. Removing this growing point signals the plant to produce more shoots and it will begin to bush out. If you have not already done so, remove the leaves halfway up the stem. As the top begins to fill out, continue pruning until the desired shape and size is attained.

Appendix 2

LAVENDER CLASSIFICATION

In recent years, lavender names and classifications have changed. If you have an older reference, you will notice a difference in the following classifications.

Within the genus *Lavandula* are six sections.

1. Section *Lavandula*

In this section are those lavenders commonly called English. They are the most winter hardy and some feel the most fragrant.

Species within this section are:

L. *angustifolia*
L. *latifolia*
L. *lanata*

2. Section *Stoechas*

Just off the Mediterranean coast of France is a group of islands called Iles de Hyeres. Once they were known by the Greek name *Stoechades*, from which this lavender gets its name. Most of this section comes from the Mediterranean region, with some from Asia Minor, North Africa, and

Algeria. It is this group of lavenders which is believed to have been used by ancient Greeks and Romans.

They are beautiful plants characterized by sterile bracts, wings or rabbit ears at the top of the flower heads. The plants in this section hybridize easily among themselves.

Species within this section are:

L. stoechas

L. viridis. Bright green foliage, with greenish-white flowers and sterile bracts that are greenish in colour. Native to south-west Spain, southern Portugal, and Madeira.

3. Section *Dentata*

These lavenders are characterized by leaves which are noticeably toothed. The sterile bracts are much smaller than those found in the *stoechas* section.

4. Section *Pterostoechas*

The name *pterostoechas* means *winged spike*. These lavenders are found in temperate and tropical Atlantic Islands, part of Africa from Somaliland to Nigeria, and in the Mediterranean area. In general, the plants in this section are heavily branched. The leaves are complex and beautiful. These are not frost hardy.

Species within this section are:

L. buchii

L. canariensis

L. minutolii

L. multifida

L. pinnata

L. pubescens

L. rotundifolia

5. Section *Chaetostachys*

Native to central and southern India. Rare in cultivation. Species within this section are:

L. bipinnata
L. gibsonii

6. Section *Subnuda*

Native to South Arabia and tropical Africa. Rare in cultivation. This section had eight species.

L. aristibracteata

Appendix 3

LAVENDER SOURCES AND FARMS

CANADA

Growing-Lavender.com
Information on growing and using lavender.

Cottage Scents
Mail order only.
Dried lavender from France, essential oils,
sachets, plants occasionally. Free catalogue.

116 Belsize Drive,
Toronto, Ontario M4S 1L7

(416) 485-5907
www.cottagescents.com

The Fragrant Garden
Mail order.
Perfume concentrates, essential oils, lavender
wands,
bulk herbs and flowers.

646 Ballyduff Road,
Pontypool, Ontario L0A 1K0

(705) 277-3934
thefragrantgarden@bellnet.ca

Mille en Fleurs
Joy Magwood
Lavender flowers, fresh and dried; wreaths; floral arrangements.
Lavender Festival mid-July.
Visitors by appointment.

1281 10th Conc. West,
R.R. #3,
Puslinch, Ontario N0B 2J0

(905) 659-3219
torrylane@worldchat.com

Botanical Specialties
Herbert Strobl
Pick your own lavender. Lavender essential oil.
P.O. Box 3009
Cultus Lake, BC V2R 5H6

(604) 824-2833
hbstrobl_botanicals@telus.net

Claybank Farm Lavender
610 Boothe Road,
Naramata, British Columbia V0H 1N0

(250) 496-5788
www.claybankfarmlavender.com

Emily Creek Herb Farm
farm address: Kawartha Lakes Rd. 24,
mailing address: 9 Clifford Drive,
Dunsford, Ontario K0M 1L0

(705) 793-3276
www.emilycreek.ca

Happy Valley Lavender Farm
3505 Happy Valley Road,
Victoria, British Columbia V9C 2Y2

(250) 474-5767
www.happyvalleylavender.com

Humber Nursery
8386 Hwy 50, R.R. #8,
Brampton, Ontario L6T 3Y7

(905) 794-0555
www.gardencentre.com

Lavender Harvest Farm
R.R. #1,
Oliver, British Columbia V0H 1T0

(250) 309-0993
www. lavenderharvestfarms.com

Mason Hogue Gardens
3532 Durham Rd. #1,
R.R. #4,
Uxbridge, Ontario L9P 1R4

(905) 649-3532

Niagara Herb Farm
1177 York Road,
R.R. #4,
Niagara-On-The-Lake, Ontario L0S 1J0

(905) 262-5690

Okanagan Lavender Farm
4380 Takla Road,
Kelowna, British Columbia V1W 3C4

(250) 764-7795
www.okanaganlavender.com

Richter's Herbs
357 Highway 47,
Goodwood, Ontario L0C 1A0

(905) 640-6677
www.richters.com

Veseys
(this is a Canadian seed company that sells a variety of flower and vegetable seeds. They carry lavender seeds for *L. angustifolia* 'Munstead,' *L. angustifolia* 'The Lady' and *L. angustifolia*)

PO Box 9000,
Charlottetown, Prince Edward Island C1A 8K6

(902) 368-7333
www.veseys.com

UNITED STATES OF AMERICA

Goodwin Creek Gardens
PO Box 83,
Williams, Oregon 97544

1-800-846-7359
www.goodwincreekgardens.com

Lavender Fleece
3826 N. Eastman Road,
Midland, Michigan. 48642

(989) 832-4908
www.lavenderfleece.com

Pelindaba Lavender Festival
farm address: 33 Hawthorne Lane, Friday Harbor,
San Juan Island, Washington State
mailing address: P.O. Box 2389, Friday Harbor,
Washington 98250

(360) 378-4348
www.pelindaba.com

Purple Haze Lavender
180 Bell Bottom Road,
Sequim, Washington 98382

1-888-852-6560
www.purplehazelavender.com

Sequim Valley Lavender Plants
184 Coulter Road,
Sequim, Washington 98382

1-888-999-3421   (360)-681-3000
www.sequimvalleylavender.com

Somona Lavender
420B Tesconi Circle,
Santa Rosa, California 95401

(707) 523-4411
www.somonalavender.com

The Sawmill Ballroom Lavender Farm
29252 Hamm Road,
Eugene, Oregon 97405
(541) 686-9999
www.sawmillballroom.com

Well-Sweep Herb Farm
205 Mt. Bethel Road,
Port Murray, New Jersey 07865
(908) 852-5390
www.wellsweep.com

Willow Pond Farm
145 Tract Road,
Fairfield, Pennsylvania 17320
(717) 642-6387
www.willowpondherbs.com
• home of Pennsylvania Lavender Festival in June

GREAT BRITAIN

Badsey Lavender Fields
Badsey Fields Lane,
Badsey, Evesham, Worcs WR11 5EX
01386 832124

Downderry Nursery
Pillar Box Lane
Hadlow, Tonbridge, Kent TB11 9SW
01732 810081
www.downderry-nursery.co.uk

Norfolk Lavender Ltd.
Caley Mill
Heacham, Norfolk, Great Britain PE31 7JE

0870 243 0147
www.norfolk-lavender.co.uk

Jersey Lavender Limited
Rue de Pont Marquet,
St. Brelade, Jersey JE3 8D8

01534 742933
www.jerseylavender.co.uk

AUSTRALIA

Australian Lavender Industry
They have an informative Web site at:
www.lavenderaustralia.com

Bridestowe Lavender Estate
Tasmania

03 6352 8182
No Web site at publication. e-mail: lavender@tas.quik.com.au

Coonawarra Lavender Estate
P.O. Box 134,
Penola, South Australia 5277

0419 247 149
www.coonawarralavender.com.au

Yuulong Lavender Estate
Farm address: Yendon Road, Mt. Egerton,
Mailing address: 58 Sharrocks Road, Mt. Egerton,
Australia 3352

(03) 5368 9453
www.ballarat.com/yuulong

FRANCE

Most of France's lavender is grown in the region of Provence. Visit from early July to the end of August, ideally before the harvest, to see the fields at full colour. On the Internet try: www.provenceweb.fr/e/mag/terroir/lavande.htm Look under "Where" for a list of lavender farms.

Write to:
Les routes de la lavande
2 avenue de Venterol,
BP 36 26111 Nyons Cedex
France

Appendix 4

LAVENDER FESTIVALS

Dates have a way of changing, so please check with organizers when making plans to attend a festival. These festivals were found on the Internet and I apologise that most sites did not give a phone number for contact.

CANADA

Mid July

Langford Lavender Festival
Langford, British Columbia,
on Vancouver Island.
www.langfordlavenderfestival.com

August

Mayne Island Lavender Festival
Mayne Island, British Columbia
www.lavenderscenterprises.com

Early July

Okanagan Lavender Farm Harvest Festival
Kelowna, British Columbia V1W 3C4
(250) 764-7795
www.okanaganlavender.com

Mid July

(Torry Lane) Mille en Fleurs
Puslinch, Ontario. North of Hamilton.
(905) 659-3219
torrylane@worldchat.com

UNITED STATES

Mid July

Pelindaba Lavender Festival
San Juan Island, Washington State
www.pelindaba.com
(360) 378-4348

Mid June

Pennsylvania Lavender Festival
Held at Willow Pond Farm.
www.palavenderfestival.com

Mid June

Somona Lavender Festival
Somona Valley, California
www.somonalavender.com
(707) 523-4411

Appendix 5

THE LAVENDER BAG

Produced twice a year is a newsletter called *The Lavender Bag*. Its purpose is to keep lavender growers, sellers, and gardeners abreast of new research and happenings. Subscribers are world-wide and the articles reflect this. A must for the lavender aficionado. It is available by subscription from:

Joan Head
The Lavender Bag
6 Church Gate,
Clipston on the Wolds,
Keyworth, Nottingham NG12 5PA UK

www.headfamily.freeserve.co.uk/lavender/
newsletter.html

BIBLIOGRAPHY

Bremness, Lesley. *World of Herbs*. London: Ebury Press, 1990.

Cavanagh, Dr. Heather. "Conference Abstracts." *The Lavender Bag*, November 2001: 16.

———— "Recent Developments in the Science of Lavender. Conference Abstracts." *The Lavender Bag*, November 2001: 16.

Dayagi-Mendels, Michal. *Perfumes and Cosmetics in the Ancient World*. Tel Aviv: Sabinsky Press Ltd., 1993.

Festing, Sally. *The Story of Lavender*. Sutton Leisure: Heritage, 1989.

Fischer-Rizzi, Susanne. *Complete Aromatherapy Handbook*. New York: Sterling Publishing Co. Inc., 1990.

French, Jackie. *Book of Lavender*. London: Harper Collins: 1993.

Gattefoss, Ren-Maurice. *Gattefoss's Aromatherapy*. Saffron Waldon: The C.W. Daniel Company Ltd., 1993.

Lawless, Julia. *Essential Oils*. New York: Barnes & Noble Inc., 1995.

Lyman-Dixon, Anthony. "Did the Tudors Invent Lavender?"

The Lavender Bag, November 2000, May 2001, November 2001: 14, 15, 16.

Manniche, Lise. *An Ancient Egyptian Herbal.* Austin: University of Texas Press, 1989.

McLeod, Judyth A. *Lavender Sweet Lavender.* Kenthurst: Kangaroo Press Pty. Ltd.: 1992.

McNaughton, Virginia. *Lavender. A Grower's Guide.* Oregon: Timber Press, 2000.

Ognyanov, I. Bulgarian. "Lavender and Bulgarian Lavender Oil," *Perfumer & Flavorist,* Dec. 1983–Jan. 1984: 8.

Price, Len. "Essential Oils from Lavenders and Lavandins." *The Lavender Bag*, May 1966: 5.

Schofield, Joan. "Lavenders in My Life." *The Lavender Bag.* May 2000: 13.

ORDER FORM

If you are unable to purchase *Growing Lavender* from your local bookstore send your order by mail as indicated below (please print), or telephone:

Mail to: Cottage Scents
116 Belsize Drive
Toronto, ON M4S 1L7
(416) 485-3566

Payment: CDN $18.95 per copy
US $14.95 per copy

Shipping: Include $2.50 per book for shipping and handling. Books will be sent surface mail unless otherwise arranged.

- - -✂ ·- -

Please send me _____ copies of *Growing Lavender*. I have enclosed a cheque or money order for _____ (made payable to Cottage Scents) including $2.50 per book to cover shipping and handling by surface mail.

Name: _____

Address: _____

City: _____

Prov./ State: _____ Postal/Zip Code: _____

Telephone:: _____ E-mail:_____